Algrove Publishing Limited
1090 Morrison Drive
Ottawa, Ontario
Canada K2H 1C2

Canadian Cataloguing in Publication Data

Faurot, Walter L.
    The art of whittling

(Classic reprint series)
Originally published: Peoria, Ill. : Manual Arts Press, 1930.
Includes index.
ISBN 1-894572-04-1

    1. Wood-carving. I. Title. II. Series: Classic reprint series (Ottawa, Ont.)

TT199.7.F37 2000   736'.4   C00-900784-9

Printed in Canada
#10800

Publisher's Note

SELDOM does a book leave as much evidence of its existence as Faurot's book on the art of whittling. You can find caged balls, wooden chains, and a variety of wooden puzzles in various antique shops across the nation. Many of these came directly from the pages of this book. It is often debatable whether or not to reprint a specific book, but the decision on this one was easy. It is a truly demanding reader who would not find the contents to be well worth the price.

Leonard G. Lee, Publisher
Ottawa
August, 2000

THE ART
of
WHITTLING

by
WALTER L. FAUROT

Illustrated by the author

THE MANUAL ARTS PRESS
Peoria, Illinois

Printed in United States of America

CONTENTS

4 CONTENTS

INTRODUCTION

THE love of tools seems to have been a natural trait among the youth of all ages. This is especially true in regard to the use of the pocket-knife. What normal boy does not love to whittle? It is an almost universal outlet for his natural creative ability; and I daresay that the boy never lived who would refuse to own a knife! Countless thousands of boys take great pleasure in aimless whittling on any chance stick or piece of wood that comes to hand. They all feel the urge to make something, though very few ever have an opportunity to learn even the elementary principles of making the many articles that it is possible to fashion with this common and highly useful tool. Few even know how to handle a knife without danger to themselves.

There is hardly a boy who does not know how to make a whistle from a twig of willow or cottonwood, when the sap is running in the spring. Beyond this point there is an appalling lack of knowledge of the various interesting things that can be accomplished.

As a boy, I became interested in the art of whittling through coming in contact with an older lad while attending a country school in the Middle West. This boy was familiar with only a few "stunts," but was an adept at those few. In the course of time I acquired an old knife and a chunk of sugar-pine, and from him learned to make a few similar things. With the passage of years I learned to make many others—some by experiment—and often I came in contact with a piece of knife work I had never seen before. Many times acquaintances, seeing my interest in such things, would describe pieces of work they had seen. Some of these I was successful in making from description alone. But in several cases it was years before I had an opportunity to actually see and study some of those things I knew only by description.

As my interest has never flagged and I have always been eager to try out new things, I am still learning. Even now, after over twenty years of experience, I occasionally run across a new idea and I do not doubt that I shall find more of them in the future. I have made, or attempted to make, every piece of whittling that I have ever heard of and many others that I have designed. Whittling, I have found, is a great breeder of patience; and many an otherwise weary hour has been whiled away in this interesting and useful occupation.

Although constantly on the lookout, I have come across but very little published work upon the subject. My information is, therefore, first-hand and everything herein described has been thoroughly tried out and found to be practicable.

Wishing to pass on the many things that I have gathered in the way of "stunts," and information regarding tools, materials, and methods, is my motive in presenting this work. Moreover, I recognize the need for practical instruction in this fascinating branch of wood-carving.

The descriptions, diagrams, and illustrations will be as clear and easy to follow as I can possibly make them. By following the instructions carefully, I am sure that any one who is at all interested can make any and every one of the articles, tricks, and novelties herein described. I can not, of course, promise you absolute success in every attempt; materials vary and accidents can easily happen while working upon a fragile bit of carving. The main ingredient for a successful repertoire of whittling stunts is perseverance. You will perhaps break many pieces before they have become finished, but do not become disheartened. Remember that this is inevitable and that breakage is almost bound to occur; then start another. Accept breaks as a part of the process. I do not intend to tell you how many pairs of scissors I broke before the first perfect pair was completed. And even now, after having made many, many pairs, I still spoil one occasionally. As it is usually my own fault, I endeavor to learn something every time it happens, and therefore do not let the failure discourage me.

WALTER L. FAUROT.

January, 1930

CHAPTER I

Tools and Materials

TO LEARN the rudiments of this fascinating craft, only the few following things are required:

A desire to create—born in us all.

An ordinary amount of patience and care. Skill will develop itself.

A good pocket-knife or two, and a small oilstone to keep them in perfect condition.

Some scraps of wood of the proper kinds, which will vary according to the nature of the article you are planning to make.

A coping- or fret-saw, which is a handy accessory and will save much labor in the blocking out of articles, especially the animal toys.

I will endeavor to lead you step by step, through all the elementary problems, and explain as clearly as I can the many quirks and kinks; also the pitfalls of the process. Many additional facts you will learn only through your own experience. But, by following the directions faithfully, you should soon become expert in carving all the ordinary subjects. You may, perhaps, fail many times in trying to carve the more difficult things; but, as I have stated before, you must not lose faith in yourself. Study the instructions and the plates again and try to discover the reason for your failure. Then get a fresh piece of wood and try again. You will soon have an envious collection of your own handiwork, which will be of more value to you as time goes on. I have a few bits which I whittled about fifteen years ago and, although they are crude in comparison to some of the later pieces I have turned out, I am sometimes surprised that I did even so well.

Woods

In order to proceed, you will need some pieces of smooth, straight-grained cedar, soft white or sugar-pine, or basswood. These woods are the best, and you will soon learn the peculiarities of each and can tell upon sight the kinds that will serve you best and which are the most appropriate for the purpose at hand. Different kinds of work require different woods. Those that I have mentioned, however, will be found practical for almost every piece you may wish to make.

After you have learned the rudiments of the craft, you can experiment with the harder woods and may eventually acquire a preference for that kind.

For the ordinary articles, which will be described first, you should have a piece of wood that will split straight and smooth, and be soft enough so that it will not crack open ahead of the blade and spoil the work. It must, at the same time, be strong enough to hold itself together after you have carved away the major portion of it. A piece of material that is found to be impossible for one thing may do very well for something else. Make a practice of saving every likely piece of wood that you come across. You will be almost sure to need just that very piece some day, and often a block of odd or peculiar shape will suggest something that it can be turned into. I have seen some beautiful work turned out from impossible-looking raw material.

Pocket-knife

The next step, and one of the greatest importance, is to get a smooth, keen edge on your knife. I have two knives that have stood the test of years, Plate 1, Figures 1 and 2. The knife shown in Figure 1 was purchased nearly fifteen years ago and is still as capable of taking and holding a fine edge as the day it was new. The two sharp-pointed blades I have always kept well polished and as keen as a razor. Indeed, that is the test they must pass before I will consider them satisfactory. After honing, whetting, and stropping them, I moisten a small spot on my forearm and, if the blade shaves cleanly and without pulling, I deem it to be sufficiently sharp for careful, accurate work. Of course, for the ordinary utility or heavy duty blade, I put on an edge that is not so fine and therefore better able to stand up under heavy cutting.

It is always best to keep one blade, usually the largest and heaviest one, for the heavier cutting and trimming. This blade, though intended for hard work, should be kept free from nicks and have, at all times, a good, keen, cutting edge.

Another test for your delicate blades is to hold a sheet of paper vertically, between thumb and forefinger, lightly rest the blade upon the top edge of this and about an inch away from your fingers, and draw the knife downward and toward you, with a slicing stroke. If the knife is sufficiently sharp, the paper will cut cleanly and easily; if dull, the paper will tear or remain uncut. The thinner the paper, the sharper the knife will need to be.

No one can tell you how to select a good knife. It is almost impossible to tell by merely looking at a knife whether it will take and hold an edge that will be fine enough for your purpose. If you can afford it, get a first-class knife to be used for whittling only. You can't go far wrong by purchasing a medium-priced knife of standard make. Any good cutlery shop should have just about what you want from around $2.00 up. A three-blade knife is the most practical. At least one of these should be the size and shape of the small ones shown in the chart diagram of my own knives, Figures 1 and 2, Plate 1.

If you are unable to procure the exact style you wish, and are forced to use almost any knife that happens to be handy, you are unfortunate. But even though this be the case, try to make the best of the tools you have, and it will not be long before you will find some opportunity for bettering matters, especially if you are sincere in your liking for the work.

Figure 3, Plate 1, shows another very handy little tool which, though not absolutely necessary, will be found of great benefit when making some of the articles. The construction of this tool will be described in the chapter on pliers.

Sharpening the Pocket-knife

For sharpening, you should have an Arkansas stone, although a fragment of an old razor hone is sometimes very good.

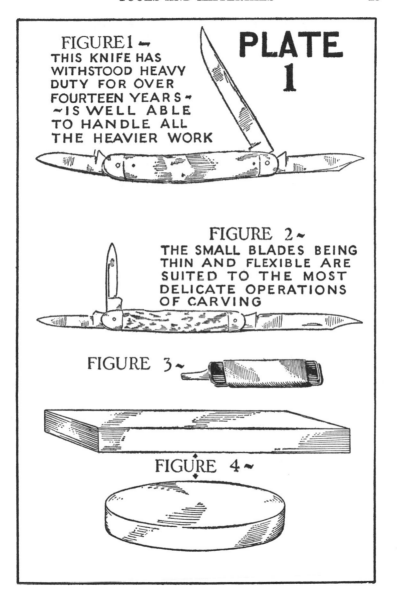

PLATE 1

FIGURE 1 ~
THIS KNIFE HAS WITHSTOOD HEAVY DUTY FOR OVER FOURTEEN YEARS ~ ~IS WELL ABLE TO HANDLE ALL THE HEAVIER WORK

FIGURE 2 ~
THE SMALL BLADES BEING THIN AND FLEXIBLE ARE SUITED TO THE MOST DELICATE OPERATIONS OF CARVING

FIGURE 3 ~

FIGURE 4 ~

For all ordinary sharpening, a medium stone will do; but for the fine, keen edge necessary in executing careful, intricate work, the whetting should be finished on one of fine texture. This will insure a smooth edge, free from "wiriness" or "pull."

Oil the stone with some light, clear oil or a mixture of kerosene and olive oil.

Hold the knife-blade obliquely across the stone in the manner shown in Figure 1 in the text. In this way you will get a longer bearing on the cutting bevel than if the blade were held straight across the stone. The back of the blade should now be slightly lifted to give a proper bevel. Merely honing with the blade lying flat would have no effect upon the edge. Next draw the blade back and forth the long way of the stone, taking care that the same angle is maintained in both directions. After a few smart strokes turn the blade over, raise the back to the same angle and repeat the fore and aft movement. The rotary motion, so commonly used to sharpen a knife, is not as good as the straight backward and forward strokes. It is almost impossible to keep the same angle and as a result the bevel will become rounded and therefore will not be as keen. The way I have described is the method used by the best mechanics. After you think you have the blade honed enough, clean the oil from it and test for the wire edge. If it has been sufficiently honed, the edge will have become thin enough to turn

FIG. 1

over slightly one side or the other. Draw the edge slantingly across the thumb and you can feel this roughness, though you should be able to see it clearly.

To Remove Wire Edge

To remove this burr, use the fine stone, if you have one. The removing can be done on the coarser, though perhaps less efficiently. Use the same method as before, only shorter and lighter strokes. As a finishing touch, I prefer raising the blade to a slightly higher angle and giving a last, light stroke on each side. This adds an extra, though minute, bevel, and is sure to eliminate the last trace of "wire." To remove any microscopic roughness and give the blade a perfectly smooth edge it should next be stropped on a strip of oiled leather. An old razor strop will serve admirably. A strip of oiled basswood also makes a neat finisher. As a final measure, you can strop the blade on the palm of your left hand. Take as much care with it as you would with a razor and the result will be an exceedingly keen blade.

The edge can be tested in several ways. With your back to a window or light, hold the blade vertically before you and look at the edge. If the edge is in any place distinct, like a thin, white line, it is still dull. If it is perfectly keen and smooth, you will be unable to see it distinctly. The wider this white line, the duller the blade.

Drawing the ball of your thumb lightly across the edge, at right angles to the blade, is another test. If the blade is sharp it will have a slight pulling effect. But if your thumb slips easily over the edge, it is still dull. Drawing the thumb-nail lightly along the blade, Figure 2 in the text, will tell you if there are any nicks. A feeling of friction, with no nicks, shows that it is sharp. If it slides easily in spots, or even for the entire length, it needs more honing.

Keep your knife clean and free from rust. An occasional drop of oil on the springs and pivots will keep them working freely and add to the life of the knife.

Figure 4, Plate 1, shows two types of hones. The diagrams are drawn about two thirds the best size. The oblong is to be preferred to the round.

Never trim your finger nails, or sharpen lead pencils with your favorite blade as that will remove the edge very quickly. Cutting paper or card-board is another use to be avoided.

FIG. 2

CHAPTER II

PUZZLE
No. 1

ONE of the simplest of the many articles possible to make, is the puzzle illustrated in Figure 1, Plate 2.

Procure a stick 12 to 14 inches long, Figure 2, and dress it down until it is about ⅜ or ½ inch square. Cut into six equal lengths and on five of these pieces cut notches, as shown in Figure 3, *a, b, c, d,* and *e.* The sixth piece *f,* remains as square and smooth as it was originally in Figure 2.

Now, if the notches have been properly cut, the puzzle will go together perfectly and form a tight, solid cube as in Figure 1.

Putting the puzzle together is done as follows: Hold piece *a,* Figure 3, in the left hand with the notches uppermost. Place piece *b* against *a* as shown in Figure 4. Next place piece *c* on the other side of *a* and parallel with *b.* The three then appear as in Figure 5. Next, lay the pieces *d* and *e* across piece *a* and against pieces *b* and *c*; being sure that the third notch is upright on both, as in Figure 6. Piece *f,* the key, can now be pushed through the hole formed by the notches in the other five pieces, making the puzzle complete, as shown in Figure 1.

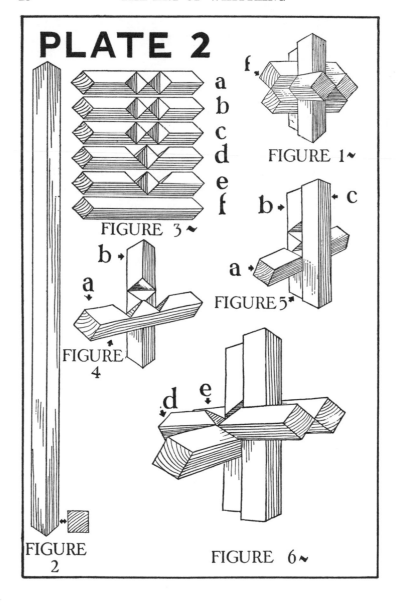

PLATE 2

a
b
c
d
e
f

FIGURE 3

f

FIGURE 1

b   c

a

FIGURE 5

b

a

FIGURE 4

d   e

FIGURE 2

FIGURE 6

CHAPTER III

Puzzle
No. 2

A RATHER neat puzzle, and one that will afford considerable amusement for its maker, is the one shown in Figure 1, Plate 3. This is a very simple trick to turn out, and all that will be needed is a piece of straight-grained basswood about 6 inches long, ⅝ inch wide and ¼ inch thick. Cut this in two pieces. The slender shank in the center should be square as shown in Figure 2.

Shape the second piece as shown in Figure 3. This piece has only a square hole in the center and all the sides of this hole will be beveled as shown in the sketches above and below Figure 3. The diameter of the hole in the second piece must be a trifle larger than the shank of the first piece, but much smaller than the greatest width of the pointed end.

When you have carefully shaped the two pieces, soak in water for an hour the one containing the pointed end. To prevent its floating and to make sure that it becomes thoroughly saturated, wrap in a wet rag and place in enough water to keep it wet. This will soften the wood to almost the consistency of cork. When you are sure that it has soaked through, place the pointed end of the first piece in the hole of the other. It can be pushed or driven through.

If the first piece is too large it is liable to split the other. If you see that too much force is required to

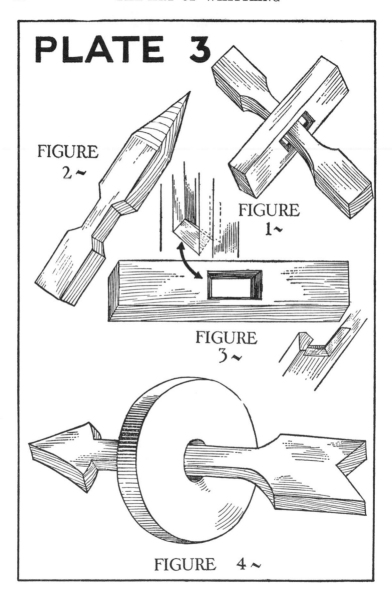

PLATE 3

FIGURE 2 ~

FIGURE 1 ~

FIGURE 3 ~

FIGURE 4 ~

put the pieces together and you are afraid that the wood is going to split, shave off a bit from the edges of the first piece until it will go through without undue strain or fear of breaking. After going through the hole, the wood will expand to almost its normal size and original shape. You should then cut off the pointed end to correspond with the other, and the trick is complete.

Very few persons will ever be able to guess how this has been done.

Variations of style and shape, using the same principle, will no doubt occur to you. One interesting form is made by using a round piece of hard wood instead of the shape in Figure 3. This can easily be made by sawing a disc from an old shovel handle, curtain pole, or other round stick of wood, and drilling a hole through the center. Or you may saw a layer from the end of any square piece and round it with your knife. This disc should be ⅜ inch, or more, in thickness. It can also be made in the shape of a heart, which is perhaps more appropriate to match the arrow form of the other half. This disc design is shown assembled in Figure 4.

CHAPTER IV

THE CHAIN

ONE of the most interesting things that can be made with a pocket-knife is the chain. This will require a good straight-grained stick, perfectly square, and any length you wish. For practical purposes, and until you understand the method thoroughly, I would advise using only a short piece, say 6 or 8 inches in length. This will allow room enough for several links; and, when you are able to make a few links and make them well, you will be able to carve chains of any length desired. Ten or twenty links offer no more difficulties than two or three. We will assume that your piece of wood is ⅝ inch square. This size will be found the most convenient. It gives plenty of room in which to work and when completed the chain is not too large and clumsy.

Figures 1 and 2, Plate 4, show pieces of wood marked out for the preliminary cuts. There are two ways to do this, Figure 1 being perhaps the easiest. Figure 2 will give you wider links from the same size piece of wood. Try them both and you will no doubt form a preference for one or the other.

After the preliminary blocking out is completed the steps following will be identical in either case.

To proceed with Figure 1. The dotted lines show the four, long, square strips that should be removed, leaving the stick in the cross-shaped form shown. After preparing the stick as shown in Figure 1 or 2, you

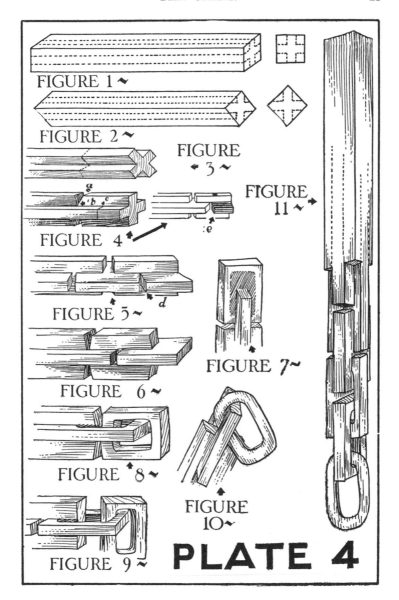

FIGURE 1 ~

FIGURE 2 ~

FIGURE ~ 3 ~

FIGURE 4 ~

FIGURE 11 ~

FIGURE 5 ~

FIGURE 6 ~

FIGURE 7 ~

FIGURE 8 ~

FIGURE 10 ~

FIGURE 9 ~

PLATE 4

must decide upon the length the links are to be. One-and-a-half times the width is a fairly good proportion, and allows plenty of room for the use of your knife.

Mark off the first link on the prepared stick as shown in Figure 3, Plate 4. This will be about 1 inch back from the end. (See dotted line.) Do not mark all four sides, as only the two that are opposite each other will be a part of the first link. Now cut a small V-shaped groove at *a*, Figure 4, until the point meets the side of the next link *b*. Do the same on the opposite side.

Next, at a point even with the center of the V-shaped groove, on the two alternate sides, make a small mark and measure off ½ inch each way, as at *c* and cut similar V-shaped grooves *d*, Figure 5, until they reach the blocked link you have already prepared. The shaded portion *e* should next be cut away, leaving your stick as in Figure 6.

Now go back to the first link you prepared and mark both sides as shown by the dotted line, Figure 7. Remove the shaded portion and your stick will appear as in Figure 8.

Mark the second link in a similar manner and remove the corresponding waste material. This will allow the first link to hang loose and appear as at Figure 9. You have only to repeat this process for each link until you reach the end of your stick. But be careful, as the more loose links you have dangling, the more apt you are to twist or crush them. Be ever sure that the free links are safe from any pressure.

Trim the corners and round off the links until they appear as in Figure 10.

In Figure 11, I have shown a chain in progressive style. Beginning at one end, we have the original block. Then link by link, each step is shown, on to the finished one at the opposite end.

The Endless Chain

An endless chain can be made with very little more care and trouble. Select a perfectly grained, square, flat piece of wood and saw out or cut a ring as shown in Figure 1, Plate 5. Round links will be the easiest for this and should be marked out as indicated by the enlarged cross-section, Figure 3. It will be noted that the cross-section is not square in this case. As the links do not cross each other at right angles they will need more room horizontally than vertically.

You must take care, when laying out the pattern, that your links, when the two ends meet, will engage each other properly. That is, they must alternate all the way around the ring. Any even number of links is correct. If you do not come out even, with the decided dimension, try a link slightly longer, or more oval, in shape. Or you can overlap them more or less in order to gain or lose a link. Cutting the links out is almost the same as in the preceding chain; but I would advise blocking them all out before cutting any one link clear through. By that, I mean that you should do all the heavy cutting while the ring is all in one piece and thus avoid straining any of the delicately carved parts.

Any ornament, cage and ball, swivel or pendant, may be incorporated in this chain, if carefully designed and planned before the cutting is started. In the case of a pendant, it should be made on the long grain of the wood, by leaving a projection at the proper point, either outside or inside the circle *before* the ring is sawed out.

Carefully sever all of the links before finishing or smoothing any of them. They will then retain their greatest strength through the most critical period and, if you should have an accident, there will not be so much time and labor lost as there would be if you had finished each link as soon as it was separated from the rest.

CHAPTER V

CAGE AND BALL

THIS one is more of a novelty than anything I have yet described. It is simple enough to make and not nearly as difficult as it looks. Variations of the idea can easily be conceived, or it may be incorporated with the chain, affording relief and interest.

To start the cage, secure a square piece of wood of any diameter and the length in proportion. At first you should work a bit large, so we will say that the block is ¾ inch square and 3 inches long. Starting ½ inch from each end, lay out a diagram in pencil on all four sides as in Figure 4, Plate 5. (See dotted lines.) Cut the shaded portion clear through until your block appears as in Figure 5.

Then turn your attention to the central portion *a,* Figure 5. An enlargement of this detail is shown in Figure 6. Cut as indicated by the dotted lines *a, a,* etc., which will free the central portion and leave a bar along each corner connecting the two ends. By working carefully between the bars you can round off the ends and sides of the center block and gradually form it into a ball, or sphere, as in Figure 7.

The dotted lines, Figure 5, *b,* show how the ball lies in the original block. A variation would be to have two balls, or more, by making the cage longer.

Almost any wood will do for this, though the softer materials will usually be found best. I have made these cages from a section of broom handle, keeping

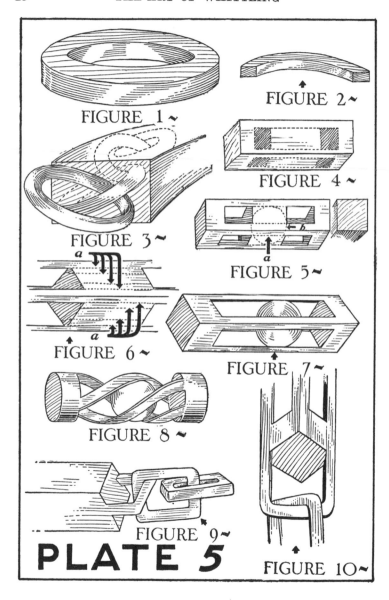

FIGURE 1 ~

FIGURE 2 ~

FIGURE 3 ~

FIGURE 4 ~

FIGURE 5 ~

FIGURE 6 ~

FIGURE 7 ~

FIGURE 8 ~

FIGURE 9 ~

FIGURE 10 ~

PLATE 5

them round and forming the side bars in a spiral. Only three of these bars were used and the result was well worth the extra effort caused by working in the harder wood, Figure 8.

To incorporate either of these methods or ideas in a chain, use either Figure 9 or 10. From the corners or across the middle of the end, a half link is formed.

CHAPTER VI

Double Cage and Ball

TO CARVE the double cage and ball, or cage and ball inside of a cage, proceed as before when making a single cage, as far as the laying out is concerned; or, as far as Figure 5, Plate 5, with the exception that the central portion should be left longer than when only a single ball is wanted. Then, instead of rounding this central core, as before, it should be squared, with the longitudinal corners appearing midway between the bars of the outer cage as in Figure 1, Plate 6. A cross section of this appears at Figure 2. When this inside portion has been made square, it will be about the same proportion, but smaller than the original piece. Then proceed as with the single cage, carving the ball from the central piece; being extremely careful while working between the bars of the outer cage that your knife-blade does not cut through them. Carefulness and accuracy will reward you with a tricky and intricate-appearing piece of work.

The finished product should appear as in Figure 3.

By making links on each end as before with the single cage and ball, this toy can be used in longer pieces. Or, placing a cage on each end of a chain makes a satisfactory finishing motive.

PLATE 6

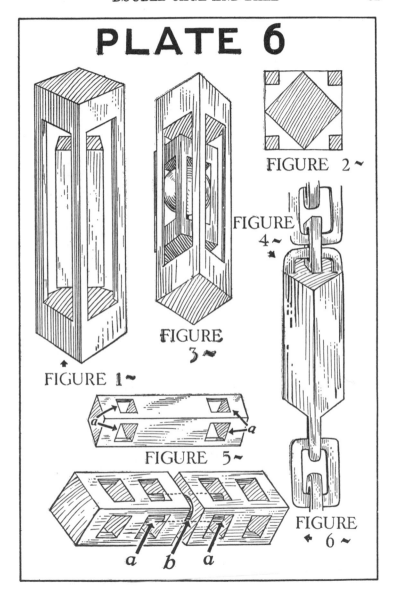

FIGURE 2 ~

FIGURE 4 ~

FIGURE 3 ~

FIGURE 1 ~

FIGURE 5 ~

FIGURE 6 ~

a   b   a

CHAPTER VII

THE SWIVEL

THE swivel is a rather interesting subject, and not nearly so intricate as it might at first appear. It has a practical value when making long chains, as it loosens up the whole work, preventing kinks and therefore accidental breakage. It also adds interest and variety to the whole, and helps to increase your repertoire of carving kinks.

Suppose that you have carved a long stick into a chain and other ornament. When doing a job of this sort it is wise to work from both ends; that is, whatever you carve at one end, make exactly the same on the other. Thus your piece will appear symmetrical and well balanced. We will assume that you have arrived within several inches of the center, with a few links of chain on each side, so that the remaining stick appears as in Figure 4, Plate 6.

Then proceed as follows: Make two square holes through the piece as shown at *a* in Figure 5. These are the same as those you made when starting the cage and ball. Next cut two more holes through the central portion, leaving only a post in the center, as shown in Figure 6, *a, a.*

Now at the point marked *b* in Figure 6, cut a groove entirely around the stick, leaving the post in the center, the same as in the two previous cuts. This post will form the shaft of the swivel. When this is done your stick should appear as in Figure 7, Plate 7. You

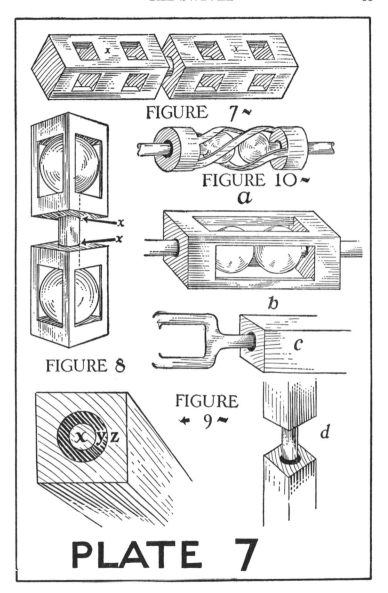

FIGURE 7~

FIGURE 10~

a

b

x
x

FIGURE 8

c

FIGURE
← 9 ~

d

x y z

PLATE 7

are now ready to form the balls from the portions
marked x, x, being careful that you do not sever them
from the round posts which you have left in the center.
The balls are formed in the same manner as when
making the cage and ball but it is not yet necessary
to trim them perfectly. Wait until all the disconnect-
ing cuts have been made and you will have more room
in which to work. Besides, the whole affair will then
revolve around itself and the trimming work will be
much easier.

Now, working carefully with the point of your knife,
carve all around the shaft at parts marked x, x, Figure 8. A cross section at the center of the piece should
look as at Figure 9; z is the outer portion of the block;
x is the shaft connecting the two balls; and y is the
part that must be cut entirely away, leaving the shaft
free to work endways through the hole in the end of
the cage. The balls, or knobs, on the inner ends of the
shafts prevent their coming out of the box, provided
that the hole y, corresponding to x, x, Figure 8, has
not been made larger in diameter than the inner
knobs. When both sides have been severed in a like
manner the shaft, balls, and boxes can be trimmed and
rounded off, giving a finished and workmanlike appearance to the whole.

Some variations of the swivel idea are shown in
Figure 10; a is the round box with three spiral bars.
The two balls are connected to the shafts, which work
freely through the end holes of the box. Or, as in b,
the box may be square. The effect of this swivel is
much the same and is perhaps easier than the other
to make. But it does not look quite as mysterious.

The shafts of *a* and *b*, Figure 10, can be joined to chains or other objects as shown at *c*. You can and will think of many different combinations of these three ideas and will soon be able to make beautiful carvings, many feet in length and with different designs and motifs along the entire length.

CHAPTER VIII

THE first item to be considered in this chapter is the sphere, ball, or other similar shape, with a smaller ball on the inside. This one no doubt originated with the Chinese, who carve some very intricate pieces from bone, ivory, and stone. I have seen a filigree ball, made from ivory, and with as many as eleven spherical shells nested one within the other. The largest was about the size of a billiard ball and the smallest little larger than a pea. Such a carving would take a vast amount of time and skill to make, as well as some very small and especially constructed tools. We, however, are only dealing with work which is possible to carve with a pocket-knife and a few simple tools, and must be content with more elementary designs and materials.

For the initial attempt, I would advise working rather large, as it will be much easier and the percentage of broken pieces will therefore be lessened. I will assume that you have prepared a round ball of wood and are ready to begin. This ball should be not less than an inch and one half in diameter, of smooth, even grain, and fairly tough in texture. You should experiment in the harder woods occasionally; such as ash, oak, maple, etc. I do not advise the use of walnut for any work that is going to be fine, such as chains or the ball and cage, as it splits too easily for small work. But, for some of the larger, heavier objects and for bas-relief carvings, there is nothing better. It takes a beautiful finish.

A good plan to follow, when starting a piece of work that is rather complex and tedious, is to use a harder wood. While the labor involved in the carving is more than when using a softer wood, the danger of the wood splitting or the tool slipping is not so great and your chances for success are amplified. And, when you finally do get the job finished and polished, it will last for a long time and be well worth the extra time, care, and effort. Do not be in too great a hurry. This applies whether you are using hard or soft woods but, as the harder wood takes a great deal longer to finish, one is apt to rush the job along. Be content with small shavings. Never pry out chips by resting the knife-blade against some other part of the carving unless you are positive that the pressure will not be sufficient to split the material. But a good rule is, don't do it!

To return to the ball you have prepared. I have shown one in Figure 1, Plate 8, with a simple design drawn upon it. A star is first drawn on each end as in Figure 2. (By end, I mean the end of the grain.) Five lozenge-shaped spots are then drawn around the surface of the sphere, leaving 3/16 inch of space between them at the nearest points.

In Figure 2 I have shaded the portions which you are to cut away to a depth of $\frac{1}{4}$ inch. Smooth off the surface of the inner portion, following the contour of the original ball so that, if you were to cut away the pattern, which is now in relief, you still would have remaining a smaller ball.

Now you can begin the undercutting of the connecting bars by working with the blade held at an angle, as shown in the cross section of the ball, Figure 3, Plate 8. The shaded parts indicate the portion which must be cut away through the apertures formed by the design. When entirely severed around the circumference of the inner sphere, the inner ball will then be free to revolve and can be easily trimmed and formed into any shape you desire. Or, if you are confident and fairly skillful, as you should be by this time, you can proceed as before and carve another ball inside the second one. But this time it will be more difficult, as you must work through two holes at the same time and be extremely careful that your knife-blade is not coming in contact with the work at any place except the point. It might be well to dull the blade except for ¼ inch or so at the extreme point. This will prevent its cutting at unfortunate places in case you are not watching each move with particular care. And as one seldom, if ever, uses more than the point of a blade in small carvings, it is hardly necessary to have the blade sharp at any other place.

You need not follow my design. Work out your own, if you wish, using windows of any different shape you may fancy. Only take care that they are not too close together so that the structure will be weak and delicate. And if the holes of your design are too large, the original spherical shape will be lost and it will not have the appearance of ever having been a ball. It is better to have smaller holes and more of them, than to have a few and these too large.

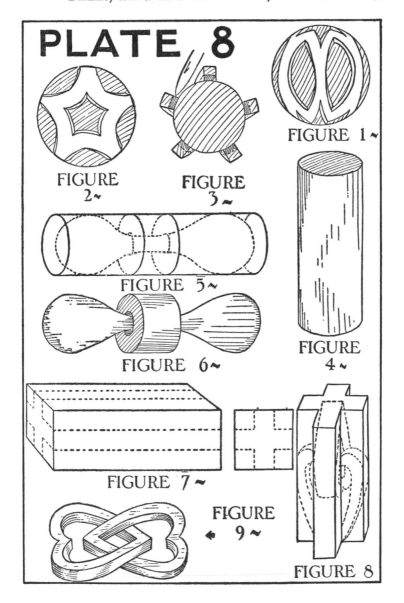

PLATE 8

FIGURE 1 ~

FIGURE 2 ~

FIGURE 3 ~

FIGURE 5 ~

FIGURE 6 ~

FIGURE 4 ~

FIGURE 7 ~

FIGURE 9 ~

FIGURE 8

Ring and Dumb-bell

Next comes the ring and dumb-bell. I designed this piece, using the elementary principles which you have already learned. It is a simple bit to make and when completed, mysterious to the un-initiated. Any small scrap of wood (hard wood is preferred for this piece) is first turned into a cylindrical shape as in Figure 4, Plate 8. The length and diameter make but little difference this time. However, about the same proportion as is shown in the diagram is convenient. The dotted line in Figure 5 will give you an idea of the cuts to make, and Figure 6 shows the finished article. The ring when cut loose will revolve freely around the shaft of the dumb-bell. The ends, or knobs, can be formed into various shapes. By making the knobs into balls, you can utilize the former lesson and cut smaller balls inside them. The idea can also be incorporated in a chain or combined with many of the other stunts to form pleasing and interesting variations.

Interlocked Hearts

Next come the interlocked hearts. The principle is the same as the chain, with the exception that the links are heart-shaped instead of round, square, or oval.

Take a square piece of wood, of almost any kind. Walnut will do very well for this, as the construction should be strong. Block it out the same as when commencing a chain. This step is shown in Figure 7, Plate 8. Figure 8 shows the block ready for the next cuts, which are indicated by the dotted lines. When completely cut out, the hearts will appear as in Figure 9.

CHAPTER IX

W E WILL now undertake what is, so far, the most intricate as well as the most interesting piece of work yet attempted, namely pliers, a completed pair of which is shown in Figure 1, Plate 9. Make them in proportion to about 3½ inches long. You can, of course, make them as much larger as you wish; and you may perhaps find a larger pair much easier to construct. But the one shown is the size I prefer and usually make. After all, size has but little to do with it, and you can experiment until you eventually hit upon the right scale to most conveniently fit your style and method of working. I have upon occasion made them much smaller—one pair, in fact, being less than an inch in length. They were excellent replicas of my regular size and perfect in every respect. I have even heard of them being successfully constructed from a parlor match!

How to Make the Special Tool

In cutting pliers, I do not use the pocket-knife exclusively. For the small diagonal cuts of the joint I find it more convenient to use a small, special tool, which can easily be made from a sliver of safety-razor blade and a couple of small strips of fibre or hard wood, Figure 3, Plate 1. This little tool will prove very handy, and several others can be made in the same way, with their edges ground to different shapes.

To make such a tool, secure the blade of any safety razor, the longer the better. Hold it firmly between the jaws of two large pairs of pliers and break off a narrow sliver of steel the proper width and running the entire length of the blade. Take care while breaking the steel that you hold your hands beneath the table top, or in such a position that when the brittle metal snaps and pieces fly, as they are very apt to do, your eyes will be protected from the flying fragments. You may have to break several blades before getting a piece of suitable size and shape.

Having obtained one to your satisfaction, there are several methods of preparing the mount or handle. You may take a strip of tough fibre or bakelite, a scrap of which should be easy to find in any shop where there are junked radio parts. Having selected the strip and cut it to size and shape, lay the blade upon one side in the position wanted and scratch its outline on the surface of the material. Then with your knife dig out the pattern formed, deep enough so that when the blade is again laid in place it will be countersunk with its topside level with the surface of the material. Now lay another similar strip of the fibre or wood on top of the blade and bind the whole together from end to end with an even layer of fine wire (copper preferred) in much the same way that you would wind a coil.

Now, stick the projecting end of the steel into a small potato. This not only keeps the steel cool and prevents it from losing its temper while soldering, but forms a convenient handle while you are doing so. Solder the entire surface of the copper wire and smooth it down afterward with a file and fine emery cloth. You can

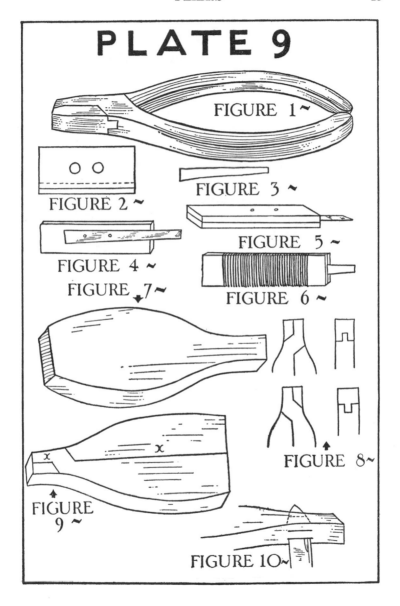

PLATE 9

FIGURE 1 ~

FIGURE 2 ~

FIGURE 3 ~

FIGURE 4 ~

FIGURE 5 ~

FIGURE 6 ~

FIGURE 7 ~

FIGURE 8 ~

FIGURE 9 ~

FIGURE 10 ~

next grind or whet the blade into any desired shape and sharpen on an oilstone. Details of the construction of these simple tools are shown in Figures 2, 3, 4, 5, and 6, Plate 9. The blade in these diagrams is the one most successful for working the pliers, and also scissors, which will be taken up in a later chapter. Upon the width of this tool depends almost wholly the size of your pliers. I should say that a trifle over one sixteenth and less than one eighth of an inch would be about right. If you find the width too much you can, of course, grind the blade narrower. It will be found well to grind it thinner than it was originally so as to offer the least resistance to the wood, but not so thin that it will break easily. Another method of mounting the blade is to take a small center-punch and, laying the blade on a block of hard wood, punch a couple of tiny holes through the metal. Punching toward the end grain will be much better than on the side. Next, shape two pieces of thin, tough fibre or hard wood to form a convenient handle and drill these at the right spots to match the holes you have punched in the steel. The pieces of wood can then be riveted together and will make a serviceable handle. Or, you can solder the blade directly to a piece of metal, first sticking the steel into a piece of raw potato, as previously described.

To return once more to the pliers. Your material this time should be a piece of very soft, smooth-grained wood, either soft or sugar-pine, pink cedar, or basswood. The latter is the best that I have found for the purpose. It must be soft enough to take the thickness of the blade without splitting beyond the edge. The size may be near $3\frac{1}{2}$ inches in length, $1\frac{1}{4}$ inches in width and 7/16 inch thick. Shape it roughly, as shown in Figure 7, Plate 9. Next mark the pattern on top, bottom, and both sides, as shown in the four views in Figure 8. By experience I have learned that certain cuts must be made before others and, if you follow the proper sequence, you will find that the most dangerous are made first while the wood is still unweakened and better able to withstand the bulk of the blade being pushed through. And, besides, each of these cuts will later on be a guide to following cuts. At Figure 9 is shown a diagram with the two most important cuts indicated by the heavy lines x, x. If the wood is going to split between the two inside ends of these two cuts, it is better that it do it now than later, in order that you do not waste any more work than is necessary.

Next, take the small special tool you have made, or the tiniest, thinnest knife-blade, and make the two cuts shown in Figure 10. These should go the entire way through, as shown by the dotted lines in the diagram. Next, using the small tool, and inserting it at x, Figure 11, Plate 10, push it on the angle shown by the dotted line, through the wood until it meets the end of your first cut, x, Figure 9, Plate 9. Do the same on the other side, only cut in a parallel direction, until it meets the end of the cut which separates the jaws. These cuts must be parallel and kept the same distance apart as the sides of the jaws between points marked x on dotted line in Figure 13, Plate 10.

Now, with your knife, make the two cuts shown by the dotted lines in Figure 12, being careful that you go no deeper than the cuts made in Figure 10. Turn the piece over and do likewise on the marks on the opposite

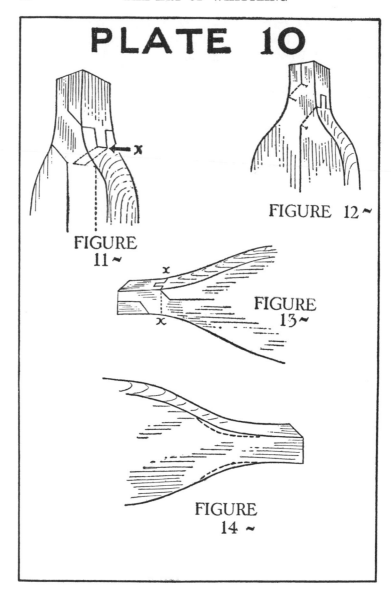

PLATE 10

FIGURE 11 ~

FIGURE 12 ~

FIGURE 13 ~

FIGURE 14 ~

side. Then take your thin blade and carefully go over
all the cuts, being sure they meet the ones they should,
and no farther. If all the cuts are loose and have
been made properly, the joint should now open freely,
and all that then remains will be to trim out the handles
and shape them in general. But never try to force the
jaws apart. If at first they do not open easily, go over
all the cuts again. If you then find they do not open
because the angles of cuts in Figure 12 are wrong, the
job can sometimes be saved by trimming a little from
both sides, as shown in the dotted line in Figure 14.
This will make the joint narrower and give more free-
dom to the parts which may have been too tight. Take
only a little off at a time, until the jaws finally open;
for, if you cut them too narrow, the joint will be too
loose. Experience will teach you the proper angles and
the right proportion to make all cuts. When finished,
sandpaper, and you will then be ready to tackle the
scissors. The joint in these is much the same, though
a little more intricate, owing to the fact that the blades
open differently from the jaws of the pliers. The
handles of the scissors will require a lot more work
than do those of the pliers, as they have finger rings
instead of the long, curved handles of the pliers. Otherwise, they are almost identical and no harder to make.

CHAPTER X

Scissors

FOR the construction of the scissors, you will need a carefully selected piece of soft pine or basswood about 1¼ inches wide, 3½ inches long, and 5/16 inch thick. This thickness, of course, is a little more than is necessary, but you will need a margin of safety when carving and can trim away any surplus after the joint is made.

In Figure 1, Plate 11, I have indicated by a dotted line just how the pattern should be marked off on the block. Figure 2 shows the block trimmed away even with this pattern. You are now ready to indicate the cuts that are to be made. Figures 3 and 4 show by the dotted lines where each of these cuts is to be made.

The sequence of cuts, which in this model must be strictly adhered to, is of vast importance. I have marked them in the exact order in which they are to be cut; that is a to m, Figures 3 and 4. The cut a can best be made with the special tool you used on the pliers, it being thin and narrow and not so apt to split the wood as the knife-blade. The cut a goes entirely through the pattern from top to bottom. Figure 5 shows the tool while making this cut. Be sure to cut no farther toward either end than the limit shown by the dotted line.

Next, make cuts numbered b and c. There is no difference which of these two is made first. They are also to be made with the little tool in the manner shown

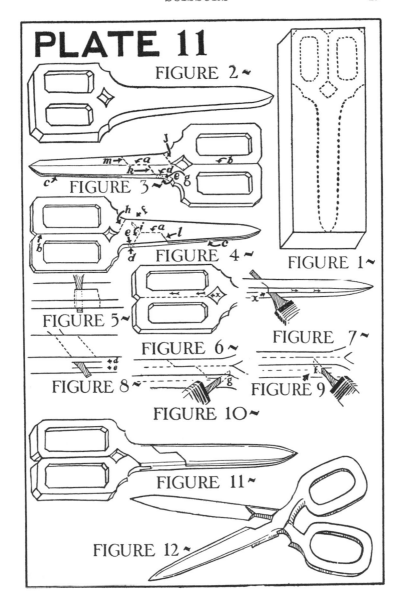

PLATE 11

FIGURE 2 ~

FIGURE 3 ~

FIGURE 4 ~

FIGURE 1 ~

FIGURE 5 ~

FIGURE 6 ~

FIGURE 7 ~

FIGURE 8 ~

FIGURE 9 ~

FIGURE 10 ~

FIGURE 11 ~

FIGURE 12 ~

at Figures 6 and 7. Insert the tool through the wood at the points shown in the diagram and cut toward either end, as the case may be. Directions are shown by the small arrows.

The cuts *d* and *e* come next in importance. A diagram of this cut is shown in Figure 8.

Shown in Figures 9 and 10 are the cuts *f* and *g*, and you must be very careful with these. Much depends upon their angle, or direction, which must correspond with that of *h*, *i*, *j*, and *k*, Figures 3 and 4. Push the tool evenly into the wood in the direction indicated and be very sure that you go no farther than the cuts *a* and *b* which you have already made. You can easily determine this depth by measuring with the blade, marking directly on the steel with a sharp, soft pencil the distance the blade has penetrated into the wood. When the tool has again been inserted into the wood and this mark is level with the surface, you will know that you have gone far enough. Too far, especially with cut *g*, will weaken one blade of the scissors and they will be almost sure to break at that point before the job is completed.

The next cuts are *h*, *i*, *j*, *k*, *l*, and *m*, Figures 3 and 4. They are all of an equal importance and there is no difference in the order in which the cuts of this group should be made. Cut them slowly either with the knife or special tool, as you prefer. Be very careful not to go any deeper or farther into the material than any other of the cuts that have been made so far.

Now, when the thirteen cuts have all been made, go over them again until you are sure that the wood is perfectly severed at all points where two or more cuts intersect. You can easily tell when you insert the tool near the intersections. If the wood springs apart slightly and appears to be free, you can be almost certain that the cuts have been properly made. If any cut appears tight and the crack does not widen slightly when the blade separates the wood, go over it once more or until you find where it is binding. When the entire joint has been loosened, and you are confident that all parts are actually disconnected, you will be ready for the try-out. Hold both handles and very carefully attempt to separate them slightly. Watch closely all parts of the joint and, if they bind in any place, you will easily determine just where it is tight. When all parts have been properly cut the joint should open freely and you can then trim the whole into a perfectly shaped pair of scissors.

If the joint is too tight to open, as sometimes happens, you can nearly always save the job by trimming slightly on the two sides as explained in the chapter on pliers. This has a tendency to make the blades narrower and decreases the radius of the joint. Such trimming, however, is not good practice and should hardly ever be resorted to. A little more care at the beginning of the job will make such a course unnecessary.

Figure 11 shows the block with all the cuts properly made. Figure 12 is a drawing of the complete scissors. A little sandpapering is all the finishing they will need, unless you prefer to wax them. This, as well as other finishing processes, will be covered later.

CHAPTER XI

Building in Bottles

THE bottle stunts, of all the whittler's tricks, are the most puzzling and mystifying to the un-initiated. Seeming impossible, they are very simple when you know how; and I now propose to show you the secret. One often hears people say, while looking at a ship or other article in a bottle, "They must have blown the glass around it," or, "They first cut a hole in the bottom of the bottle, insert the ship, etc., and weld the glass back in place." They are wrong in both instances. To do either would be impossible, as any glass worker can tell you. The method that really is practiced is so easy that it is possible for anyone to achieve marvelous results with no knowledge whatever of legerdemain, mysticism, or glass blowing.

Selecting a Bottle

Your first consideration will be to select a bottle of pleasing shape, of clear glass, and having a neck which is not too small. I should say that a bottle of one quart or one fifth gallon in size is about the best. At least, it is the size most commonly used for this sort of job. One can generally obtain for a small sum at any drug store a bottle that will be satisfactory.

Figure 1, Plate 12, shows a few styles or shapes of bottles and necks that are suitable. Choose a subject that will best fit the shape of the selected bottle. Before making any design, be sure that you can get all of the

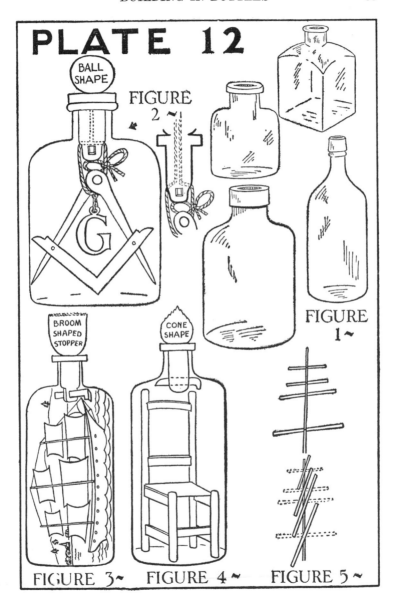

PLATE 12

BALL SHAPE

FIGURE 2 ~

BROOM SHAPED STOPPER

CONE SHAPE

FIGURE 1 ~

FIGURE 3 ~   FIGURE 4 ~   FIGURE 5 ~

component parts of it into the bottle you have elected to use. Some of the things can be made in one piece, others will have to be constructed in several parts.

Make a Drawing

To begin, you should first trace the outline of the bottle upon paper. Then draw an inner line to allow for the thickness of the glass. Next sketch inside of the diagram of the bottle a design of the subject desired. You will then be able to scale any part so that it will be small enough to pass easily through the bottle's neck. The wood used should be old, dry, sound, and close grained. A fairly hard wood is best as it will not be so apt to warp or split. Never use cigar boxes, as the wood is coarse grained and splits too easily. Pieces of old, broken furniture are sometimes good. The wood will be well seasoned and is usually of excellent quality.

Never design two or more bottles exactly alike. Variation can be secured in the size of the inner objects, the subject matter, color and kinds of wood used, shape and style of stoppers, size of the bottle itself, etc.

Colors and Finishes

Cords and ribbons should be pretty and the bowknots should be tied so they can never shake loose. Cords may be gilded, but ribbons never. Jap-a-lac is easily obtained and is very good. You can get silver, gold and aluminum, and every color of wood stains. Mahogany and rosewood look the best but it is sometimes advisable to leave the wood unfinished and in its natural state. When painting, give each coat plenty of time to dry. Stick a pin in each piece and tie a thread to it. Dip into the varnish and then hang up to dry, and drip. After painting, pieces should never be touched inside of twenty-four hours unless you are using brush lacquer, which dries in a short time. After the piece has been varnished and has hung for about an hour, a big drop of varnish will form and hang at the bottom. Touch a piece of wood or rag to this and it will come off. The use of the quick-drying brushing lacquers is sometimes employed. But they destroy the identity of the wood, which shellac or varnishes do not do.

Gold, silver, and aluminum paints must be applied with a small brush. These are best for the parts that require bending as they are flexible and can stand hard usage. Take pains to shape each part neatly, truly, and symmetrically—the square parts square, the round parts round, and every center exactly in the middle. The bottoms of bottles are seldom flat, consequently your bottom pieces must be arched to fit, or else the whole design must stand upon its corners. If a piece is to be constructed to fit the bottle when lying in a horizontal position, you must, of course, fit the curve of the glass perfectly; or, in the case of ships at sea, fill with putty, which will remove that difficulty.

Perfect Joints

All joints must fit perfectly. Lay pieces in position and mark with a sharp knife. In the case of pieces which cross and must have a hole through them, hold them together in the correct position and bore the hole through both at once. Pieces that mortise and tenon together should fit snugly but go together easily, as very little force can be used once they are in the bottle.

In addition to your knife you will need a hack-saw, a drill, and a file; also some stiff wires bent in various ways to go through the neck of the bottle and hook, hold, pull, or push the parts about. Hammer and flatten the end of one wire until it splits. This will make a tool for holding the little wooden pins and placing them properly in their holes. Another wire must be flattened on the end and then filed or ground to an edge similar to a knife-blade. This will be used to reach inside and cut off threads. A long wire can be doubled in the middle so as to form a pair of tongs with which to reach inside the bottle and hold or squeeze the parts together. A wooden rod, $\frac{1}{4}$ inch square, with a notch cut in one end, will be found handy in turning screw-eyes; and two such pieces will serve to open out parts that have been bent or rolled. Large wires bent and flattened will be found necessary for modeling and shaping putty. Always complete your design, varnish it, and put it together as a tryout before placing any of it in the bottle. Be sure that it suits you and that all parts will go together freely and easily. When it fits together to your satisfaction, take it apart again and re-assemble piece by piece inside the bottle.

Order of Inserting in the Bottle

Study out the proper order before inserting any of the parts. Pieces that require much attention should go in first so that others will not be in the way.

In Figure 2, Plate 12, the G goes in first because it is the hardest piece to open and flatten out. Next the square goes in and the G is drawn up out of the way by the cord that belongs to it.

A Ship in a Bottle

In Figure 3, the land is made first. The trees, houses, and other objects are stuck into it. Then the entire ensemble is painted and allowed to dry and harden for several days before the putty that forms the water is put in. The hull is the next piece to enter. Allow it to set and harden several days more, when it will be time to rig it with the masts and sails. In Figure 4 the back is assembled first, then the sides and seat. And so with every design that you make, there is a special and proper order for assembling.

If at any time you should lose patience, drop the work for awhile. In due time you will get it all together. At times you will need someone to hold the bottle and some of the many threads while you are using both hands to manipulate a few of the others.

Figure 3, showing the ship design, is about the most interesting and beautiful of the many bottle designs one can make. There are several methods for the construction of ships, the simplest being shown in Figures 1 to 5, Plate 13.

The hull of the ship in Figure 3, Plate 12, is made in one piece, which must, of course, be small enough to pass freely through the neck of the bottle. Drill holes at the proper places, about 1/4 inch in depth, in which to step the masts. The yard arms are to be pivoted to the masts with small lengths of pins, so that they will fold into a long, narrow bundle, as shown in Figure 5, Plate 12. Short pieces of pins with the heads projecting slightly along the sides of the hull are admirable for looping the ends of rigging over. Rig the yards and masts completely, using small loops at the end of every yard and stay that joins the hull. These can be hooked or unhooked at will. All rigging lines should be made taut and the thread will stretch enough to allow your doing this. Where the rigging joins the bowsprit it can be hooked to small wires; or the bowsprit can be made separate and stepped into the hull, at will, after the manner of the masts.

Put a small drop of glue in each hole before stepping the masts. Wait until the first mast is set thoroughly before assembling the second, and so with each of the following.

The hull need not be shaped like a hull beneath the water line as it will be sunk into the putty and be concealed below that point. By leaving the bottom flat and driving a few tacks part way into the wood, with the heads projecting slightly, the putty will hold the hull absolutely tight.

To make the ocean and land, take common putty and roll into long cigars small enough to pass through the neck and long enough to cover the inside area of the bottle. Press several of these together to form the land. A block of wood dropped inside and pressed on hard by a strong, bent wire, will flatten out the putty, where a wire alone would prove unsuccessful. Cut and shape the putty into beach and hills. Paint it green or other desired colors. Then stick in the buildings, trees, and other objects which have been previously made and painted. You may have to make the larger buildings in several parts, doweled together. The

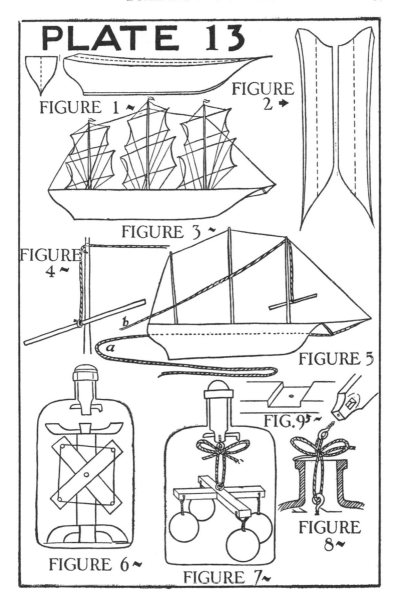

PLATE 13

FIGURE 1 ~

FIGURE 2 ~

FIGURE 3 ~

FIGURE 4 ~

FIGURE 5

FIG. 9 ~

FIGURE 6 ~

FIGURE 7 ~

FIGURE 8 ~

largest ones should be the nearest to the shore, the smaller ones farther away. This gives perspective and an illusion of distance and makes the scene more real-istic.

When all these are dry, you can put in the putty for the water and shape it into regular waves. In all this putty work never allow any of it to touch the inside of the bottle where no putty should be, as it will soil the glass and spoil the effect. The neck is not so important as it can easily be swabbed out, or it can be protected by a cone of paper while inserting the putty cigars.

Paint the waves, and while the putty is soft assemble the hull and press it down hard into the putty. It looks better to give the vessel a slight list to one side as though it were under a heavy breeze.

The masts, sails, spars, and rigging all go into the bottle at once, then the masts are stepped, singly, as before described.

For larger and more elaborate ships, make the hull in several pieces, being sure that the joints are accur-ately made and that they will join together smoothly and neatly. These parts must be doweled together and assembled inside the bottle. One way to do this is to carve the hull from a single piece of pure straight-grained wood, then split into sections small enough to pass through the neck. Set the dowels in these parts without further trimming.

The "Trick Hull"

A trick hull is shown in Figure 1, Plate 13. The hull is split as shown in Figure 2. A very slender groove is next cut the entire length of both halves at the position shown by the dotted lines. In order to match these grooves perfectly so that the two will combine and form a single hole running the length of the hull when the halves are assembled, take a piece of thread and dampen it slightly with ink or rub with a soft lead pencil. By pressing the two halves of the hull together, with the thread between them at the exact position where you will require the groove to be, you will get a mark upon the wood which can be followed easily. On this line, on both blocks, make a small groove only large enough for the easy passage of a thread when the two pieces of the hull are glued together, as you may now proceed to do. To be sure that no glue has entered the groove and thus clogged it, leave the thread in place until the glue has partly set. Then pull a few inches of the thread through. This will clean the hole and thereby prevent the thread from sticking fast. The thread should be linen of the kind that is commonly used to sew leather, or the heavy kind known as button thread. These can be obtained from any department store or from a shoemaker. The thread should be of ample length, say two or three feet; and, after the glue is set, tie the two ends together so that they can not accidentally slip from the hole before they are needed.

The Rigging

Next make the rigging and assemble it completely, except that, in this case, the masts should be pivoted permanently to the deck in such a manner that they will lie down lengthways with the vessel. Each spar and yard, instead of being pivoted to a mast, should have a hole bored through its center; slightly larger than the head of the pin which is to be sunk firmly into the mast. Drill a small hole through each mast head for the threads used in hoisting the yards to pass through. Rig all the yards and masts in the manner shown in Figure 3, Plate 13, making all connections permanently to the hull. Tie a stout thread to the center of each yard. Lead the end up through the hole in the mast head and leave it long enough to reach well outside the bottle. This is shown in Figure 4, Plate 13. Next untie the thread that runs through the hull and lead the forward end out over the bowsprit, and up and back through the hole in the foremast head. Pull all the slack through except about one foot, as shown in Figure 5, Plate 13. Then put a clove hitch around the mast head and lead the thread to the next mast. Repeat the process until you have connected all the masts at the proper distances. Now fasten the thread firmly to the stern. Try it out and see that it works properly. Lay all the masts down flat. Hold the hull in one hand and pull the long thread. If the masts rise into their proper positions easily, as in Figure 5, Plate 13, your work is correct.

Then see if the yards will hoist and hook neatly over the pinheads. When everything is arranged nicely, fold up the ship and it will be ready to insert, leaving all the projecting threads sticking out of the bottle. Follow previous instructions for setting the hull in the putty. When it is thoroughly dry and set, pull the thread a, Figure 5, which raises the masts into their proper positions. Drive a small wooden peg into the hole in the stern where the thread emerges, first dipping in glue. This holds the thread fast without further attention. When dry cut off both thread and peg flush with the hull.

Next, with the aid of your wire tools and thread *b*, draw the foreyard up and hook over its proper pin. Rig the farthest mast first, then the next farthest, etc. After hooking each yard in its proper place, the thread used in hoisting it may be snipped off and withdrawn.

While this method requires more work at first, it is much easier to handle the job on the inside of the bottle than some of the assembling plans, and it makes a neater job. A small drop of paint should conceal the peg at the stern.

There are several other bottle designs which, while they are not strictly whittling problems, should, I think, be included in a work of this kind. Figure 6, Plate 13, shows the simplest design that looks well, and it is best in very small bottles. Make the dowels separately and glue into holes drilled into the post and other parts. Put a drop of good glue on each dowel as you assemble in the bottle. Put the bottom cross-pieces in first and press them together with a rod. Then push in the lower dowel of the post. Next put the middle cross-pieces on their axle and push down the cotter pin to hold them. A drop of glue on the half-lap joint will hold it perfectly. When dry, hitch the end of some bright-colored thread, yarn, or cord by a slip-knot over one of the four pins. Then push the arms around to wind the thread upon the pins until their lengths have been covered. Next put a drop of glue where the thread touches, to hold the last end. Let this stand aside for several hours to allow the glue to harden; then cut the thread off close with the sharp wire tool.

Now you can put on the upper cross-piece, with glue on this dowel, also. Insert the stopper with its cross-bar, and all is complete. The trick stopper is explained on pages 67 and 68.

Figure 7, Plate 13, is a very easy and pleasing design. The cross frame is halved out at the center as in Figure 9, and the eye-wire screwed through both pieces of the frame at once.

Drop the lower piece into the bottle first after you have tried out the joint and made a hole for the screw-eye. To insert the upper part with its eye-wire and cord into the bottle, you will have to screw the eye-wire all the way in so as to get the piece through the neck. Once inside you can unscrew it again to let the lower piece come into place. Then it can be screwed through both pieces. The balls make it hard to rest this frame upon the bottom of the bottle in order to work upon it, so two blocks of wood can be dropped in for it to rest upon. Or a wire tool can be made to hold it while assembling. Screwing the upper eye-wire into the stopper is clearly shown in Figure 8.

Figure 1, Plate 14, is very easy and the explanation is shown in Figure 2. Put the cord or baby ribbon through the ball first, fasten to the eye-wire and tie the proper length in a tight bow underneath.

Now roll the ball up tight and have someone tie a cord around the middle. Work it smaller if you can and then have your assistant wrap the upper half with a strong basting thread, after which the binding cord can be taken off.

A funnel of paper in the neck, Figure 2, keeps the friction of the rubber from holding to the glass, thus

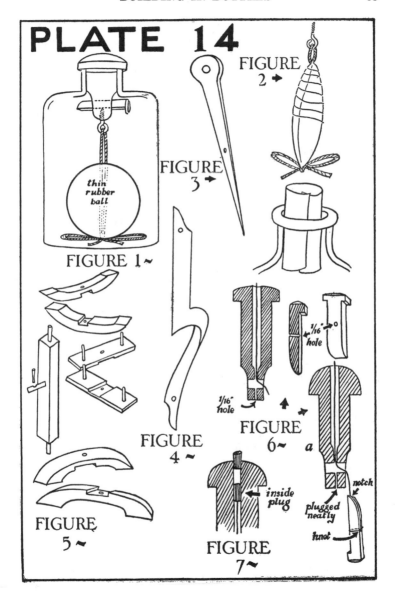

PLATE 14

FIGURE 2 →

FIGURE 3 →

thin rubber ball

FIGURE 1 ~

FIGURE 4 ~

1/16" hole

FIGURE 6 ~ a

1/16" hole

inside plug

notch

plugged neatly

knot

FIGURE 5 ~

FIGURE 7 ~

letting the ball slip easily inside, after which the thread can be cut and the ball allowed to expand. The eye-wire can now be screwed into the stopper.

Always bronze the ball before putting it into the bottle. You can use different shades of bronze for variety, or draw maps on the ball to represent a globe.

The Mysterious Cross-bar

Figure 2, Plate 12, is a very popular design that all Masons will want, and it is not hard to construct. In this piece there is not only the mystery of the cross-bar, but the cord that passes through the stopper above the cross-bar and ties to the G under the compass in a hard bow-knot.

Bore the hole for this cord clear through the stopper and just above the square hole of the cross-bar. Have the cord come through right where the shoulder of the bottle begins. Cut into the stopper a little on each side, so as to allow for the thickness of the cord as shown in Figure 2, Plate 12. This drawing does not show the cross-bar in place, only the square hole; but a cross-bar goes in there, as in all the designs.

Make the compass out of hard wood, each half cut like Figure 3, Plate 14. These halves are held together by a small round-headed screw, cut short enough, and the whole gilded.

The square and G are made of thin lead. Hammer out a piece of lead pipe until it is as thin as medium-weight cardboard, then rub it on a piece of sandpaper until all marks disappear. Cut it to shape, gild, and it is ready to insert.

Tie the cord to the G first, then bend it on both sides just enough to go through the neck. Straighten and flatten and smooth after it is once inside the bottle by using two notched sticks.

Next gild the square, bend it as shown in Figure 4, Plate 14. Drop it inside and open it out flat by means of wooden rods, or pieces of wood dropped in to press upon. The two holes in the square for the screws must be made small enough to hold the screws while assembling. Drop the screws, which have also been gilded, into their holes by means of a notched stick, then press them into the holes made for them in the legs of the compass.

The holes in the compass must be made large so the screws may be pressed in easily. A large drop of glue or bronze solution in each hole will hold the screws if left alone until dry and hard. Now put in the stopper, cross-bar, and cord. Explanations of this process are to be found below. This design looks best when gilded over cord and all.

Figure 4, Plate 12, is very attractive and not difficult. The seat is made of leather or velvet, glued to the top pieces of the sides. This allows the seat and both rails to be rolled up and passed through the neck.

Make the back of the chair to fit tightly in the bottle. But the seat should not quite reach the glass, so as to have room to get the tenons into the back part. Put the back together first, with glue on every tenon as they go together. The sides and seat are easily assembled after a little study.

Plate 14 contains, at Figure 6, the illustration explaining the trick stopper. The secret consists of boring a small hole all the way up through the stopper, and a similar hole through the cross-bar at the center, counter-sunk on the lower side to hold a knot on the end of a waxed thread, Figure 6.

Make a slight notch on the top end of the cross-bar, just enough to hold the thread temporarily and not be noticed afterward. Press the thread into this notch, then pass it into the square hole mentioned on page 66, up through the stopper, and out at the top.

Now, drop the thread and cross-bar, assembled by its point a, Figure 6, Plate 14, through the neck of the bottle. Then pull on the thread until the cross-bar enters the square hole and comes half way through the stopper. Hold the thread by one hand and press down into the hole alongside it a plug of soft wood to wedge it in permanently as in Figure 7. Cut off the thread, poke down the loose end and glue in a plug of the same wood as the stopper, with the grain running the same way, Figure 7. When the plug has become set, cut it off neatly and finish with black paint, lacquer, or dark varnish. Never leave the natural wood, for the existence of the plug and thread must be perfectly concealed or the secret will be given away. Bronze will sometimes conceal the plug, but not always. If the outline of the plug shows in spite of the paint, countersink it to make it look like a lathe mark. Acorn-shaped stoppers perfectly conceal the plug by means of the curved point into which you whittle the end. Conceal the hole in the lower end of the stopper, also, by a plug of the same wood or by an eye-wire, when the design calls for it.

When a suspension cord is used, as in the Masonic design, make a false bow-knot on the cord first, and drop it with what it holds, through the neck. Then pass the two ends through the cross hole on either side of the stopper and up through the center hole, alongside the thread and out at the top. Draw up the waxed thread first until the cross-bar is in place then hold all three ends and plug, cut, and finish as above.

The reel shown in Figure 6, Plate 13, is made in sections as shown in Figure 5, Plate 14.

Figure 8, Plate 13, shows how you should fasten thread by an inside plug. The outer plug can then be finished off better than if the thread protruded.

CHAPTER XII

FANS

THESE are at once simple to make, and the result is generally a thing of beauty which will always provide a unique decoration.

It will be advisable to start with a small fan of but few blades until you learn or acquire the knack of making them. There is hardly any limit to the size or number of blades with which it is possible to construct the fans. I have made them up to three feet in diameter and having seventy-five blades.

The wood should be soft pine or basswood. Use a piece 8 inches long, 1 inch wide, and ½ inch thick. Figure 1, Plate 15, shows the block. Measure about 3½ inches from one end and trim as in Figure 2, dotted lines. This part is for the handle.

Now, on the two narrow edges you can cut notches of different shapes and styles. Figures 3, 4, and 5 show a few variations. Sometimes by boring holes through the wide side of the block you can form nice designs, Figure 3. Then, when the blades are cut, they will have a delicate, lace-like appearance.

At points *a* and *b,* Figures 3, 4, and 5, you must always provide notches similar to those shown; so that when the blades are spread and arranged properly they will interlock and enable the fan to stay open and remain rigid. Figure 6 explains this clearly. When you have trimmed your block into a suitable design you are ready to separate the blades. Your knife should be

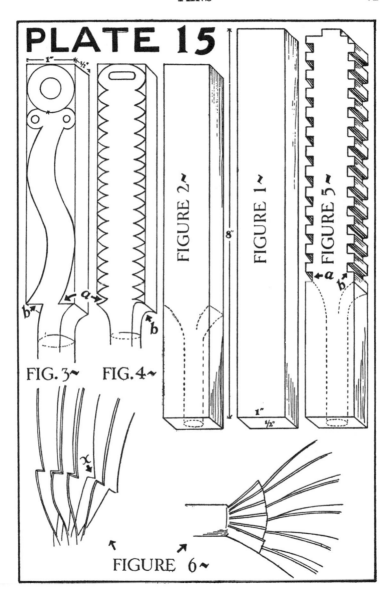

PLATE 15

FIGURE 2~

FIGURE 1~

FIGURE 5~

FIG. 3~   FIG. 4~

FIGURE 6~

very sharp, and the heavy blade is the best for this purpose. Start at the end as in Figure 1, *a,* Plate 16, and cut a shaving less than 1/16 inch thick, or as thin as is possible and still retain the shape and strength. By making a few of these shavings on a piece of waste material, you can arrive at the thickness which best suits your knife and wood. Shave this slice back as far as the spot where the handle is to begin, 3/4 inch or more past the notches *a* and *b,* endeavoring to keep it an even gauge all the way. It will curl some according to the thinness, but that can be remedied later.

When all the blades have been split, the fan will appear as in Figure 2, Plate 16. But sometimes the wood is too brittle or too soft and then you must soak it thoroughly before beginning to slice the blades. This is usually the better method, and you will find it necessary to do it, anyhow, before taking the next step. After the blades have been split and again water soaked to make them tough, collect them together at the end, and hold tightly. Take hold of the solid, or handle end, and slowly twist one-quarter turn in either direction at point *a* in Figure 3. The fan will then appear as in Figure 3. Still keeping the wood wet and pliable, begin with the center blades and carefully spread them apart. Then cross, hook, and interlock each blade as you come to it, as in Figure 4.

Lay the fan between two flat surfaces, such as a couple of boards, and allow to dry thoroughly under a weight before removing. This will eliminate all curve and warp from the blades. The handle can then be carved into any ornamental shape, and if the stick is long enough, a chain may be added.

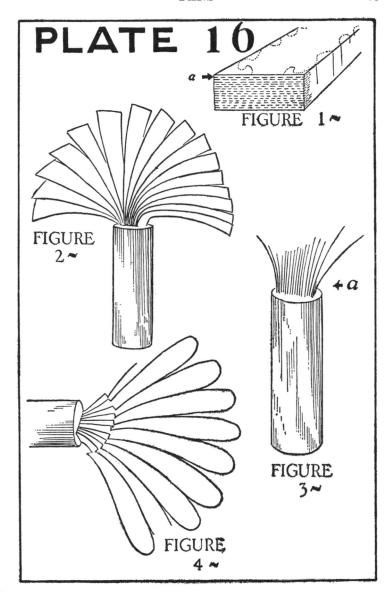

PLATE 16

FIGURE 1 ~

FIGURE 2 ~

FIGURE 3 ~

FIGURE 4 ~

CHAPTER XIII

SLIDING MULTIPLE JOINT

THIS joint is rather intricate and is a piece of carving that will test your skill and patience. But it will make an unusual centerpiece for a long chain and will be found useful in many places where elaborate embellishment is desired.

The wood in starting should be 4 or 5 inches in length and four sided, or square. Carve off the corners, making the piece eight sided as in the cross-section, Figure 1, Plate 17. All of the sides must be of an equal width. The idea, in brief, is exactly like a chain, excepting that the links are double.

Figure 2 will show you how to make the diagram upon the block. You will have very little room in which to work between the eight bars. It is well to remove first the sections a, a, in Figure 2. This is shown in detail in Figure 3. Then carve the individual bars. If half of the joint were removed, it would appear as in Figure 4. To make this still more intricate, a ball may be left on the inside. Finished cages are shown in Figures 5 and 6.

This joint may also be constructed with three bars on each side, or half—six in all—in which case, you would start with a round stick and carve it six sided, Figure 7. Proceed as with the eight barred one. In this way you will have more room to work, but the result will not be quite as strong or fine when completed.

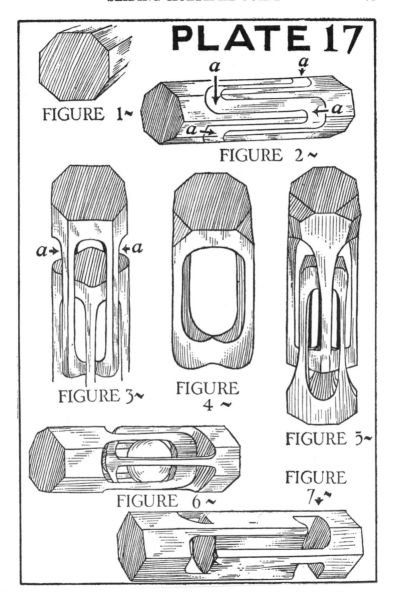

PLATE 17

FIGURE 1~

FIGURE 2 ~

FIGURE 3~

FIGURE 4 ~

FIGURE 5~

FIGURE 6 ~

FIGURE 7~

CHAPTER XIV

MULTIPLE JOINT

THIS piece is made from a single stick, marked as shown in Figure 1, Plate 18. The joint is exactly the same as the one used in constructing the pliers. Begin with the large center joint first. Great care must be exercised in laying out these joints, in order that they be at exactly the proper angle to insure the halves working smoothly. No trimming should ever be done after the joint work has been started. When finished, the piece should fold together neatly and have the appearance of a flat, squared block of wood. Trimming to make defective joints work a little more smoothly would only spoil this effect.

After the large joint has been cut, the piece will open in the manner of a pair of pliers, in the form of a cross.

Then begin with the end joints, making sure they are marked exactly as shown in Figure 2. Otherwise you will find it impossible to make the diagonal cuts on the inside as they should be. Figure 3 shows the *wrong* way to mark them out. When the five joints are completed, the piece will appear as shown in Figure 4.

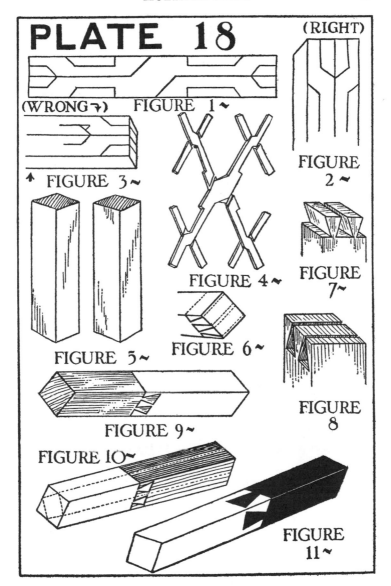

PLATE 18

(RIGHT)

(WRONG →) FIGURE 1 ~

FIGURE 2 ~

FIGURE 3 ~

FIGURE 5 ~

FIGURE 4 ~

FIGURE 6 ~

FIGURE 7~

FIGURE 8

FIGURE 9 ~

FIGURE 10~

FIGURE 11~

CHAPTER XV

Trick Dovetail Joint

WHILE purely a trick, or optical delusion, this joint has been known to fool clever carpenters and cabinet makers. It appears at its best when constructed from woods of two different colors—walnut and ash, pine and cherry, or any other dark-light combination that will give good contrast. Both pieces must be square and exactly the same size, Figure 5, Plate 18. A perfect dovetail will require especially fine carving.

It will be well to make the tongue side first. Mark one end of your block as shown in Figure 6. Cut away the surplus material until it looks like Figure 7. Now you can easily carve the second piece into the form shown in Figure 8. Test these until they go together perfectly and firmly. When you are satisfied with the joint, give it a thin coat of glue and lay it away until almost dry, or until it has reached the tacky stage. Then coat the parts again and put the joint together. Lay it away again for a day or two until it is thoroughly dry, when it will appear as in Figure 9. Now, draw a line down the exact center of each side and, with a plane, although it may be done with a knife, cut away all the dotted portion shown in Figure 10. This will make the stick square again, but with a smaller diameter.

The finished joint will look complicated enough to mystify the un-initiated, and is shown complete in Figure 11.

CHAPTER XVI

The Dogs

I DO not know the origin of the stand described in this chapter but presume it to be Oriental, as I have seen it utilized as a base for the crystal balls used by fortune tellers and crystal gazers.

For material, you should have a rather hard, tough wood, as the stand must be durable enough to bear a slight weight which comes, for the most part, where the grain is across the length of the piece. The larger part of the strain will come at the ankle and rump of each dog, as indicated at *a* and *b* of Figure 3, Plate 19, where the grain runs across the contour of the figures. The breast is the only other delicate place and, as there will be no weight above the joint, it is un-important.

Use a block 2⅛ inches in diameter and 6⅜ to 6½ inches in length. This gives a good proportion and the size is amply large for easy carving. It is not as intricate as it may look and, if you have already made the Sliding Multiple Joint described in Chapter XIII, you should have no trouble. The principle used is much the same.

You will now dress the block down until it is a hexagon having six equal sides measuring slightly less than 1⅛ inches. Figure 1, Plate 19, shows the position of the dogs in the wood. The noses start at alternate corners at the same end. The body passes diagonally through the piece to the corner farthest from its starting point.

It will be well to start whittling from the ends of the piece. At the corners selected for the heads, roughly block out the shape, as in Figure 6. Make the greatest width, at the ears, about three quarters of an inch, and this will allow plenty for the later trimming. The point of the breast comes nearly 1½ inches below the nose and you can follow through the contour at the neck to this point.

Do the same with the feet at the other end and carry them the same distance, 1½ inches, as you did the necks. The piece now will have taken on some definiteness and you have landmarks to work from. The form of the joint can then be roughly sketched in, following the plan in Figure 1. Cut away a little at a time, and as you remove a pencil line by a shaving, replace it immediately so that the plan will not be lost. Keep the members rough and large enough to allow trimming after the bulk of the waste portions has been taken out. By this time you should gradually have worked into the joint itself, and the carving from here on will be much the same as when making chain links.

Figure 2 shows a top view and Figure 3 a side view of the dogs.

When completely cut out and trimmed, they should look as in Figure 4. Figure 5, of course, shows the completed piece opened out.

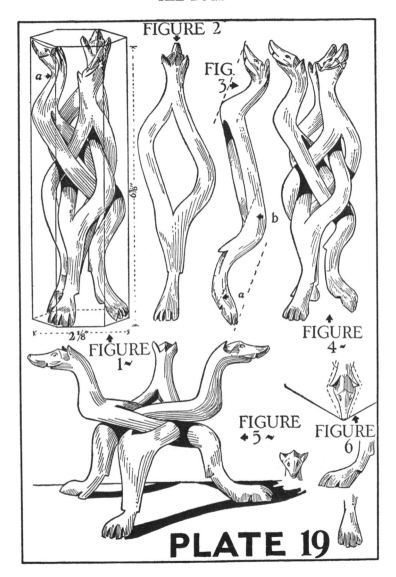

FIGURE 2

FIG. 3

FIGURE 4

FIGURE 1

FIGURE 5

FIGURE 6

PLATE 19

CHAPTER XVII

ANIMAL TOYS

THE carving of small animals has become a popular pastime, and much cleverness and latent ability have been developed in making them. Many clever silhouettes have appeared in this country, but the craftsmen of England have gone a few steps farther and are turning out animals in a more finished form than is usual here.

The start is the hardest, as you must first have a design. If you cannot draw the animal you want, keep your eyes open for good, clear pictures in magazines and papers. Such pictures usually appear in a size that is very convenient for your use. A profile or side view is, of course, desired. Lay a piece of transparent paper over the picture and trace with a soft pencil a careful outline and other distinctive features of the animal.

You should next prepare a piece of wood large enough to accommodate the drawing. For the simpler forms, a single piece of wood about 1 inch thick will do. But more success will result, if you use a built-up block for the purpose. For the initial attempt, it is best to try a subject of simple lines. A pig will do nicely as it is fat and curvy. As you will see in Figure 1, Plate 20, his body is thick and round while the legs are proportionately slender, though short. It is practical to make him from a single piece of wood and, as most of the carving will have to be done on the

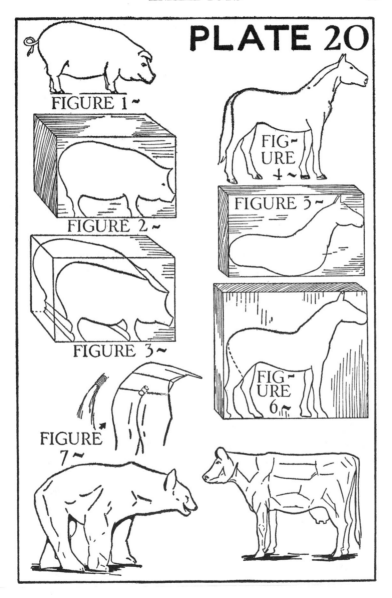

PLATE 20

FIGURE 1~

FIGURE 2~

FIGURE 3~

FIG-URE 4~

FIGURE 5~

FIG-URE 6~

FIGURE 7~

body, you should let the grain of the wood run the length of the pig. Transfer your drawing to the wood by laying the tracing face down on it. Then, with a hard pencil, holding the tracing in place, go over all the lines with enough pressure to transfer the original drawing to the wood. A piece of carbon paper could be used. But it is then difficult to place the drawing on the block in the proper place and position. With the transparent paper you can see at all times what you are doing.

After the drawing is traced on the wood, Figure 2, remove the paper and go over the lines again to sharpen them and correct them as you wish. The next step is to saw out the figure, keeping close to the outline, but on the outside, or waste side of the line, Figure 3. This is as far as many toy-makers go and, with the proper color scheme and accessories such as ears and tail, it is surprising how lifelike a mere silhouette can become.

Next take your knife and gradually round off all the corners. Frequently consult your original photo as a guide, or, if possible, a live model. Do not cut away too much at a time. If you cut too deep, it is hard to replace and not workmanlike. Trim away as much of the surplus as you like until you think the pig looks as much like a real one as you can make him. Cut the groove between the legs and round them. He is then ready for the ears which can be whittled from a thin piece of wood and glued on, or from a small scrap of leather cut from an old shoe tongue or glove. Endeavor to place the ears correctly making them look as lifelike as possible. Here, observation of a live pig will be valuable. The tail can be made from a piece of string which has been saturated with glue and wound around a pencil or round stick of the same size. When dried, cut off small sections and glue them into place in a small hole made by driving in a nail and pulling it out, if an awl is not handy.

For the built-up process, which is suitable for all the larger animals and those with long, slender legs, we will first try the horse, Figure 4. Prepare your tracing as before, either from the chart or any other picture you may wish to use. Secure three pieces of wood about ¼ inch thick. Trace the body on the piece that has the grain running lengthwise, Figure 5. Trace the entire outline on the other two pieces so that the grain runs vertical, or parallel, with the legs, Figure 6. This gives them strength and they will not break while you are working on the figure.

Saw the three pieces out, as was done for the pig. Now glue the three pieces together with the two vertical grained pieces on the outside, and place between clamps or under a weight for at least twelve hours. When the glue has set proceed as with the pig, cutting off the corners and gradually shaping the animal to the natural form, Figure 4. The ears can be made as before, but this time the tail should be more bushy than the pig's. A section of rope will do very well. Bind one end of it with thread for a small distance. Bore a small hole as in Figure 7, glue the bound end, and insert in place.

Other animals are shown in Plates 20 and 21. The method of making these is the same as described for either the pig or the horse. Remember, if the animal

PLATE 21

A
few
ideas
for
your
use

has tall, slender parts, such as the legs of a horse or a cow, you must use the built-up method to insure success. Unless the wood is very hard and tough, the legs are apt to break if made of one piece. And wood that is too tough or hard is not easy to work with and really not necessary.

CHAPTER XVIII

Finishes—Wax, Shellac, Varnish

BEFORE using either wax, shellac, or varnish, the pieces to be treated should be thoroughly clean and dry. And be sure that they are placed where no dust or dirt can collect upon them while they are drying.

Wax can be obtained already prepared in one- or two-pound cans, or it can be prepared in any quantity by using one part sliced beeswax and one part turpentine. Pour the turpentine over the wax, and heat and stir until thoroughly dissolved. When cool, apply with a brush, waste, or the fingers. Polish after an hour with a piece of flannel rag or felt. Waxed surfaces that have become soiled can be cleaned with a rag moistened in turpentine. They will then be ready for re-waxing.

Shellac is a varnish of a resinous nature and is the exuded secretion of a scale insect that is deposited on twigs of trees. In its natural state it is of a reddish or orange color, but when bleached it is known as clear or white shellac. It is best used where natural wood finishes are desired.

The first coat of shellac will dry in about five hours, and should be rubbed down smoothly with fine sandpaper before succeeding coats are applied. As many coats as you think necessary can be used, sandpapering after each coat. The final coat may be left without sandpapering, thereby retaining a high, glossy finish.

Shellac, however, dries hard and is apt to check and chip off if unduly exposed to varying extremes in temperature. Varnishes are more elastic and durable, being of a vegetable origin. Varnishes used for finishing furniture may be used and should be allowed to dry from twenty-four to thirty-six hours after each coat. Sandpaper or pumice and felt should be used to rub down each coat used.

INDEX